WHO ELSE BUT GOD

From Trauma to Triumph

Golda Hawthorne

WESTBOW
PRESS®
A DIVISION OF THOMAS NELSON
& ZONDERVAN

This book is a work of non-fiction. Unless otherwise noted, the author and the publisher make no explicit guarantees as to the accuracy of the information contained in this book and in some cases, names of people and places have been altered to protect their privacy.

Scripture quotations marked (NIV) are taken from the Holy Bible, New International Version®, NIV®. Copyright © 1973, 1978, 1984, 2011 by Biblica, Inc.™ Used by permission of Zondervan. All rights reserved worldwide.

WestBow Press books may be ordered through booksellers or by contacting:

WestBow Press
A Division of Thomas Nelson & Zondervan
1663 Liberty Drive
Bloomington, IN 47403
www.westbowpress.com
1 (866) 928-1240

Because of the dynamic nature of the Internet, any web addresses or links contained in this book may have changed since publication and may no longer be valid. The views expressed in this work are solely those of the author and do not necessarily reflect the views of the publisher, and the publisher hereby disclaims any responsibility for them.

Any people depicted in stock imagery provided by Thinkstock are models, and such images are being used for illustrative purposes only. Certain stock imagery © Thinkstock.

ISBN: 978-1-5127-9165-5 (sc)
ISBN: 978-1-5127-9164-8 (e)

Library of Congress Control Number: 2017909967

Print information available on the last page.

WestBow Press rev. date: 10/11/2017

DEDICATION

Thank you, Mom and Dad, for instilling virtues that have shaped me into the woman I am today and for raising me God's way. Thank God I have not departed.

To my sisters, Deborah and Rebecca, thank you for having a listening ear, a helping hand and kind words of encouragement, for just supporting me.

To my precious gem, Dominique, I thank God for you, everyday. You are a joy, a delight, and a wonderful gift that God has given to me.

To my heavenly angels, Aunt Iris Smith, Angela Huggins, Doreen Edwards, Dahlia Johnson, and Annette Williams, I am grateful that God has used you to minister to me throughout the early stages of my journey. May God continue to richly bless you.

And to my Bishop, Hezekiah Walker, thank you for believing in me and stretching me to become more.

CONTENTS

FOREWORD

I am so blessed to have gotten to know Ms. Golda Hawthorne. I met her at a tender age of 10 when I became a member of her father's church. He was the Pastor of Ebenezer Pentecostal Circle Assembly located in Brooklyn, New York.

She became friends with my two children who were around the same age and subsequently frequented our home. Having known her as a little child, I was impressed by her gift of song. She was very engaged in the choir and participated in all activities when asked to.

I admired her vibrant personality and jovialness over the years. I have had many opportunities to connect with Golda on both a personal and spiritual level.

Her inspiration to write this book has become her perseverance through adversities. Her love for God has inspired her to project her innermost thoughts through words.

Golda has been an inspiration to me and I know that sentiment will resonate to others.

Angela Huggins

I give honor to God for this opportunity. I have known Golda Marie Hawthorne from her birth and had the privilege of being her first babysitter. Always a bright and intelligent child, Golda let nothing deter her. She was quick on the uptake.

In one of my earliest and fondest memories of her, Golda was about five years old and we were going out. On the way to the elevated train station, we met one of my new coworkers. The woman asked me if Golda was my daughter and I said no. We spoke for a while and when a train went by, Golda said, 'Mommy, we missed our train,' needless to say, the woman thought that I was a liar.

Even when Golda lost her arm in grade school, she did not lose her determination or drive. Nothing held her back. She grew into a lovely young lady with a beautiful voice who loved to sing.

Golda was always very independent. As a young mother, she drove from Florida to New York with her baby. I admired her as she took care of her daughter. Although she lived with me for a short time when she moved back to New York, Golda did not depend on me to take care of the baby.

Golda is always thinking of what she can do next to better herself. I am extremely proud of her for writing this book that I know it will be a blessing to others.

Doreen C. Edwards
Doctor of Theology,
Doctor of Psychology of Christian Counseling

ACKNOWLEDGEMENTS

I would like to take this opportunity to gratefully acknowledge the editorial assistance and contributions of Millicent Waterman, Assistant Professor and Assistant Director of the Nyack College Writing Center, for her genuine acts of kindness.

INTRODUCTION

For years, I questioned the various adversities throughout my earlier life. But God was there all the while. He allowed these seasons of my life to occur for my good and for His glory.

What you go through in life helps you to mature and build character. Most of all, they are tests you must pass to share your testimony with others, so they can be encouraged and realize they are not alone and can also overcome.

It's not so much about you but for someone else. It's a two for one.

So celebrate your struggles, adversities, and various seasons in your life, for you are on an assignment of the Creator. When you can grasp this concept, you begin to live a purposeful life. So stop blaming your history and those in it and walk in your destiny!

'You are my treasured possession, the apple of my eye, chosen, blessed with every spiritual blessing and predestined to obtain an inheritance.'

- God

Chapter One

THE SUMMER OF '77

Clanging tambourines, beating of drums, single, double and triple clapping of hands, the strumming of guitars, a moaning saxophone, and the stroking of the organ as the saints sing, "When we all get to heaven, what a day of rejoicing....". This is one of the most familiar and pleasant memories I have of my childhood.

But for me, there wasn't much rejoicing during the summer of '77.

April 25, 1972, I entered the world. I am the first born to a charming, British yet stern Pentecostal minister and a loving, God-fearing mother. My father named me Golda after the fourth and only female Prime Minister of the state of Israel, Golda Meir, and my mother hyphenated Marie. So I was welcomed into the world as Golda-Marie Hawthorne.

In a prayer, awaiting my arrival, my father declared I'd be a child of renown. Who knew how much weight that would carry?

But God!

From birth, doctors diagnosed heart murmurs and the breaking and resetting of my joints but my father would not allow them to perform any form of surgery and prayed for divine healing and nothing much was said after that.

My parents had owned a couple of houses on the block, and I

attended private school between the ages of three and fourteen. Later I became the eldest of three siblings, all girls.

We worshipped and fellowshipped in services on Sunday. Tuesday night was prayer meeting. Thursday night was Bible study. Occasionally, early Saturday morning we had prayer service.

Having various properties, my father would help family and friends, internationally and domestically, have a temporary place to stay. My home was the equivalent to Grand Central Station. A historic commuter, rapid transit railroad terminal at the infamous, New York City landmark in Midtown Manhattan on 42nd Street.

He moved a particular family into our home that changed the course of my little life. The males in that family tampered with my body and corrupted my mind. I experienced this multiple times each week for almost a decade between the ages of five and fourteen.

Unfortunate for me, that summer I learned also how to emotionally eat and that bought on childhood obesity. That was my coping mechanism.

Even though my immediate family and church family surrounded me, I lived an isolated life tortured by secrets and flashbacks acquainted with low self-esteem, confusion, shame, anger, guilt, bitterness and the incapability to forgive.

Honestly, as a child, I thought I was the only one experiencing this turmoil and questioned myself numerous times, "Why me?" I didn't do anything to anyone to deserve this, yet I accepted this path as my destiny because it became my "norm".

But God!

I did not know it then, but God was there. In one of the general letters of the New Testament he said, "Never will I leave you; never will I forsake you." God is omnipresent, omnipotent and omniscient. He is always present, all powerful and all knowing.

Chapter Two

DESOLATE, BROKEN AND VIOLATED

You would think that event was horrific, but it was nothing compared to what was about to happen. By 1980, once again my father opened our home again. This time my torment really started!

You see there was a shift in my day-to-day life. And it wasn't a positive one. Unfortunate for me, I started to become troubled at school due to traumatic occurrences that happened in the home.

Experiencing numerous sleepless nights, one particular night weary, drained and mentally exhausted, I told my parents this individual was bothering me. My parents not totally clear on what bothering me meant, I had to relive graphic details explaining what this individual put me through night after night after night. They removed him from that part of the home but you know that wasn't the end of it. For the next three years, that portion of my life was put on pause. I experienced a hiatus.

One spring day, I stepped out my home to get some fresh air. It was a peaceful, quiet day. The windows to my home were open, welcoming the fresh, cool breeze; the sun was shining, no unwanted guest occupied our home, but I noticed the basement door to the church was open. It wasn't something out of the norm, so I called out to my father. He was the only one with the keys and would maintain the grounds.

Numerous times I would call out to him not getting a response.

So I didn't think anything about it. I entered the basement from the street, circled the premises hoping to find him, but he was nowhere in sight which was unusual. He would never leave the basement door open from the street entrance. Something told me to leave the premises, immediately, but by the time I computed that information and made the first step, I heard this loud sound.

I made a 360 turn to see where the sound was coming from. The sewer door burst open and there stood this tall large silhouette in pure darkness. My eyes dilated, my mouth dropped, and my heart stopped. At that moment, my day took a turn for the worse. The three-year hiatus was over.

There I stood face-to-face with this individual. Fear gripped me! My childhood innocence existed no more.

In the midst of this confusion, my viewpoints on life were never the same. I was encouraged to be silent after this episode. I became discouraged and withdrawn.

But God!

"What?"

-Richard M. Nixon

Chapter Three

OOPS?!?

One of my passions at the tender age of five was I always loved doing hair. My dream was to become a salon owner with all the financial benefits, on the high end, the full beauty experience – Thai massages, facials, manicures, pedicures with reflexology, waxing, saunas, Jacuzzis, aroma therapy and invigorating herbal teas. The idea was when you left you felt rejuvenated, refreshed and recharged.

I loved braiding my hair – the Dutch and the French braids. The French was my favorite. Just creating various styles from day to day. It was a delight!

By the time I was eleven, I was weaving hair (sew in more than glue in). Creating pineapple waves and mastering finger waves was my weekly enjoyment on anyone who volunteered themselves in the neighborhood.

For the first half of seventh grade, especially the beginning of winter '84, I experienced excruciating pain in my upper left arm during regular school hours. Mysteriously, when I got home, I hadn't any recollection of this pain. This would go on day after day, for a couple months.

But God!

As a child, I also had a passion for the arts and for expressing my individual style. Every night I would create a new 'do. It was just a natural part of me. One ordinary school day I created an original piece, I am not clear where I got the inspiration from but I never did that style ever again.

That day the teacher left us to do our math class work. A fellow classmate decided she wanted to play tag (in class, in a private school where you were spanked for discipline). Go figure! I declined her offer, but she was persistent. She took MY hole puncher, the one shaped like a ruler, made out of hard rubber and metal which can be hooked in your binder, and slapped me with it.

Even though she was smaller than me in stature, it felt like she had the strength of a thousand men. IT HURT! So that motivated me to retaliate. I grabbed the hole puncher from her, retaliated and was on my way back to my desk. As I turned around to walk down the aisle back to my seat, she yanked the hole puncher out of my hand and hit me on my upper left arm, the same area where I was experiencing months of excruciating pain. Well, it was a pain that could not be expressed. I screamed at the top of my lungs, expressing grave agony.

From this point, everything was foggy until my bone was reset at the hospital. To my recollection, when my mother arrived at the hospital, they updated her on their findings. They reset the bone and placed it in a cast. Yet they could not understand why the bone of a child of my stature broke so easily.

They took x-rays and found a cyst on the bone where I was fractured. My mother and I were referred to a specialized hospital for a second opinion. The doctors were not sure if that cyst was malignant or benign so they sent us to a specialized hospital.

Upon arrival, we were startled to learn what type of hospital we were referred to - a cancer hospital, a very well known cancer hospital in our city.

After taking my vitals, it was expressed that I needed to have a biopsy. In less than a year, once again, my life was going to take a turn for the worse.

But God!

Following doctor's orders, I went in to have the minor procedure.

A "mistake" occurred. The main nerve in my left arm was punctured to the point that I began to bleed internally. Doctors tried to stop the bleeding but were unsuccessful.

Coming out of surgery, I was wrapped so tightly with bandages that I thought they removed my breast, the ones that I just acquired and were getting accustomed to.

Beside that, I lost so much blood that I now needed a blood transfusion. My God. This was a time when HIV/AIDS was on the rise. From the little knowledge I gained on the subject of my little twelve years on this earth, a blood transfusion was one of the ways you could get AIDS. And I was terrified.

But God!

So, here I am, twelve years old, my body going through changes, I have access to three limbs and a dead weight (my lifeless left arm, in a cast) that I am forced to walk around with for another four months.

The first time, the young lady at school broke my bone, the bone was reset, but I had life in the arm. This time, the main nerve was cut, and I lost all forms of life and feeling.

Because of that experience, I will never live in my home again for at least another year. I became an inpatient, which was kind of bittersweet because my body would not be sexually violated for a while yet I would be butchered and treated like a "guinea pig" by medical professionals.

Forget about my junior high school education! I should be making preparations for high school. Once again I am confronted with confusion, fear, distrust and anger, to say the least.

But God!

Here I am a new resident of Manhattan, which is not a problem, but I did not imagine it like this. It would have been nicer if I experienced it like George and Weezy Jefferson with a deluxe apartment on the east side.

After the "mishap", I finally acquired a room of my own for a few nights. Then I started to acquire roommates of all ages, from one year olds to twenty-five year olds from every continent, which wasn't bad, but they all were passing away.

I had roommates almost as often as trains ran through Grand Central. It was a frightening experience, young people from all walks of life dropping like flies all around me!

By the time you began to get acquainted with one, the friendship ended–wonderful short-lived friendships. My mom was the most familiar face around except for the regular doctors and nurses.

But God!

To encourage myself, I had a collection of gospel cassette tapes. Yes, cassette tapes. I would play them on my boom box to uplift my spirit. All I had was a song.

One day flipping through the channels, I stumbled across this woman hosting her own show. She brought me so much inspiration on that hospital bed. She gave me hope. God used Oprah Winfrey, in that hour, as if to say, "I am not finished with you yet." Look what I did for her.

I needed some form of hope. Here I am, a young lady who once delighted herself in being fashionable must now be reduced to two hospital gowns worn back and front and must carry around an accessory not of choice – an IV of chemotherapy, methotrexate to be specific.

Also the hair I once stayed up hours styling for the next day of school, I now experience it shedding all over my pillow over night. I am now dazed and confused and don't know or understand everything but God is in the midst working things out for my good.

I love music of all genres. The 1980s saw an explosion of musical expertise. Artist of yesterday came back fresh and strong. New artist made their mark. As Pattie Labelle said " everyone was expressing their new attitude." Even the President was a former actor. Everybody was going for his or hers. And I was feeling the fever also. I was in my element. It was a thriving time. Whatever you wanted was in your reach. You just had to go for it.

I had dreams. Big dreams. Besides being a hairstylist, and

creating my own fashions, I had acquired sketching skills, started writing poetry and songwriting. Thoughts were flowing. For me, I was going to begin as a voice major at Fiorello H. LaGuardia High School of Music and Arts. The sky was the limit from that point on but there was an interruption; crazy scenarios just threw me off course, far beyond what I could ever imagine! Beyond what my mind could conceive!

But God!

In the book of Jeremiah, one of the major prophets of the Old Testament, the Lord declared, "For I know the plans I have for you, plans to prosper you and not to harm you, plans to give you hope and a future." You see God is the creator of all. He knew you before you were conceived in your mothers womb. Sometimes we do not understand the path panned out for us. But in the end God gets the glory and in some interesting way it was for our good. There is always someone who needs to hear your story for strength; encouragement, to remind them they are not alone and they can overcome.

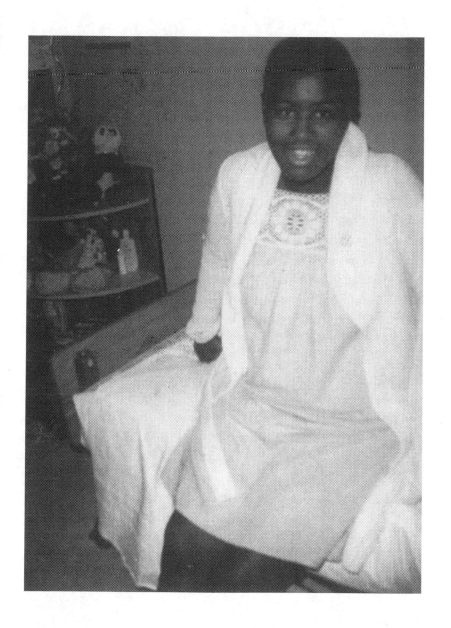

Chapter Four

SALVATION, RICH AND FREE

It is now two months in, March 24,1985, and I receive a visit from a sister of my father's church. She begins to share with me that even though my father is a minister of the gospel, and both my parents have a personal relationship with the Lord that does not cover me. She then explains to me that I am at the age of accountability. She asked me if I wanted to give my heart to the Lord because tomorrow is promised to no man.

As the Apostle Paul proclaimed, "That if you confess with your mouth, Jesus is Lord and believe in your heart that God raised him from the dead, you will be saved. For it is with your heart that you believe and are justified, and it is with your mouth that you confess and are saved." I repeated the sinner's prayer with her and began my walk with the Lord.

At that moment, I felt assured that everything was going to be all right. There was a sudden peace. Always carrying a thick-skinned persona, I actually felt a calmness and joy amidst my calamity. It was the strength I needed to take me through the day, that hour. Feeling so unsure all my life, not being able to trust authority figures that were supposed to protect me, just broken and shattered, I now felt a deep assuredness.

Chapter Five

DOOMS DAY

It is now May 9, 1985, the day my body will be disfigured permanently. Dooms day! It's still vivid in my mind. As tears run down my face, under the anesthesia, fading away, I asked the doctor if I can keep the decomposed arm after he amputated it because I did not want to part with it. I also asked him what he is going to do with it. Will I see it again? As I fade away he tells me "No. It is the property of the state."

Going under, confused again, only to understand that the doctor made a mistake and months later they erase the mistake by amputating it, leaving me disfigured, mutilated and once again, physically scarred for life. I look over at my left arm for the last time connected to my body and shut my eyes.

But as David uttered to the Lord, "For you created my inmost being; you knit me together in my mother's womb. I praise you because I am fearfully and wonderfully made, regardless of this present circumstance.

But God!

We all know the story of Samson and Delilah. Yet Samson set apart and raised to be used by God, also became disabled. Imagine a man who once tore a lion apart with his bare hands then later ate honey out of its carcass. He struck down thirty men by himself, stripped them of their belongings just to pay his debt of a solved riddle. Who caught three hundred foxes, tied them tail-to-tail in pairs, placed a torch between each pair of tails then lit the torches and set them loose to destroy the enemies goods. He then struck down a thousand men with a jawbone of a donkey.

Unfortunately, a cheap woman who nagged him for the secret of his strength compromised his destiny. She sold his secret to his enemy. They seized him and gouged his eyes out, and he was now blind.

But he had the last say. His strength began to surge again. His enemies, out of mockery, requested he entertain them. In a crowded temple, with over three thousand alone on the roof, he stood between two central pillars, bracing his right hand on one pillar and his left hand on the other, pushed with all his might and destroyed every living soul.

With me, medical professionals got creative on how they administered the medication. Instead of pricking my five fingers everyday for blood work and searching for veins to give me the IV, a broviac was inserted and connected to my main nerve. It was supposed to be cleaned everyday, manually, but I'm a thirteen-year-old going through the motions. My mother runs to and from Brooklyn to Manhattan taking care of me, my father who just had a massive stroke and my two younger siblings, so it got infected.

According to my pediatrician, all I needed was some antibiotics but the medical team sent for a pulmonologist, a lung doctor, to carve out a piece of my lung by starting the incision under my right bosom straight through to my back.

This is the same bosom where they just inserted a broviac to my main nerve. 'I guess they earn brownie points for who can sever me more.'

This is the one that broke the camels back. After administering chemo for half a year, now, suddenly, they are confused about the dosage. My height hadn't changed and my weight wasn't a dramatic loss so what was the confusion? Unexpectedly, I experienced a coma.

Immediately, they tell my mother to get the funeral arrangements together. While under the coma, I remember this dark tunnel with this pinhole light at the end of the tunnel. Curious about this light, I begin to walk towards it. The more I walked, the brighter and larger the light became. Just about to step in the light, I had a change of heart and decided to turn around. The next thing I knew, I opened my eyes, but I was a stiff in the hospital bed.

Not able to move, I could just look around mostly straight up to the ceiling and whatever is leveled above me. I thought I was alone, but I heard a sound. Not able to turn my head, I witnessed my mother, at the corner of my eye, sitting by my bedside praying. When she realizes I am alert yet tongue tied, she tells me to say, "Thank you, Jesus!" consistently until I can say it clearly. Following her instructions, I retained my speech.

With delight, she calls the doctors to report my recovery. But by the look on their faces, twelve doctors encircle my bed with looks of marvel and regret.

Funny yet sad, they gave me the impression that the "guinea pig" won't die as if this were not the result they were looking for.

But God!

That was the kind of energy or response they emitted. So how was I supposed to feel coming out of the comma?

It is now January 1986. In the fall, I am to start high school. Not just any high school but the high school of my dreams, Fiorello H. LaGuardia H.S. of Music and Arts as a voice major. Julliard was next.

Unfortunately for me, I was still an in-patient and nothing seemed to be moving forward. I had to take matters into my own hands. For once, I had to take a stand for my body and my destiny.

After a typical physical, I had a meeting with the physicians. They were neither happy nor intrigued at a 5 feet 11 inches, 13-year-old girl of color informing them of her personal discharge. They were preparing to take another year of my life to perform radiation. 'For what?'

Now let's recap. I never had cancer. They punctured my main nerve that led to a mutilation. The first year was wasted with unnecessary surgeries, a coma and daily intravenous medical procedures. And now they want to steal more of my precious life to follow through with radiation therapy. You gotta be kidding me!

Fortunately, it was so liberating, I gave them their farewells and found my way home.

Chapter Six

HOME SWEET HOME?

How do you go back to familiar territory yet it feels unfamiliar? Because of that one-year fiasco, I have to readjust to home life, life itself and finding my place again. It was so much easier in the hospital, but this was the reality of things – learning all over again to wash and comb my hair, bathe, button, and zipper my clothes. I had to decide if I was going to leave my left sleeve tucked in or simply hanging out blowing in the wind. Also I had to learn how to wash dishes, tie my laces and apply toothpaste to my toothbrush.

The list could go on. But amongst that I went back to finish my education but I haven't seen a textbook in a year. I went back to life as usual, but I was not usual.

No preparation was ever made to help me cope with my loss. No preparation was ever made for me to learn how to adjust to my new body. I just took it like a soldier and kept moving.

But God!

I can still hear my mother saying, "Golda, cast your cares upon the Lord and leave it there." But somebody was praying for me. I can still recall my father praying for all his children. He would start from the eldest and work his way down to the youngest. It sounded like he was reading through the tribes of Israel. You see, there were a dozen and a half of us, a story for another day. All positive!

But things were different on all levels. The physical, of course, which anyone could see. There was also the spiritual; I was a babe in Christ. The emotional, dealing with my thoughts of who and whose I am, convincing myself that I am still beautiful, accepting my body for what it is. Psychologically, just grasping the fact that my body was disfigured and in the past year death knocked on my door a couple times. Even worse, things really fell back into place briefly with the molester and in full swing with the pedophile. Lord! Are you there?

Chapter Seven

RAWR!!!

I didn't realize it then but I was angry. If anyone looked at me twice or gazed at me too hard, anger welled up. I didn't care if you were young, old, male, female, Jew or Gentile. Standing at 5 feet 11 inches tall, about 160lbs. and the mind of a 14 year old, I was a ticking time bomb, a fuse about to blow.

So much had happened to me in my little fourteen years on this earth and I had had enough. All you had to do is give me a reason. Fuel my fire. I needed to release years of pain, heartache, displeasure and indignation.

But God!

King Solomon said it best, known for his great wisdom, "A fool gives full vent to his anger, but a wise man keeps himself under control." God's word is so powerful and true. I could not have made it this far without Him.

Imagine this. Before birth, a death wish is put out on your life. After birth, you are separated from your biological family to spare your life. You are then adopted and raised by a princess, live in a palace yet learn that your biological family is impoverished and are treated unfairly. Who wouldn't have anger issues after a scenario like that? But Moses was being set up for something great. He was chosen for a specific purpose.

The Apostle Paul instructs us to be kind to one another, tenderhearted, forgiving one another, as God in Christ forgave you." God never said that you could not get angry but he stressed not to act out on it.

Chapter Eight

GUNPOINT

One of the girls with whom I grew up in the neighborhood asked me to meet her at her boyfriend's house after school. Being at her house on many occasions and meeting him from time to time, I never thought anything of it. The guy's little brother even went to school with me, so I didn't feel anyway. That won't happen again. LESSON LEARNED!

As planned, the next day I waited for her at the house on the stoop. That's what we did back then. Observing the passersby, I temporarily acquainted myself with fellow peers, classmates, whatever. As the day went on, it somehow appeared she was going to be a no show. But I am old faithful, such a loyal friend. My schoolmate invited me to come in the house because the day was dwindling down. They offered me something to drink. And put on Scarface for me to watch. At this point, I think I took my loyalty to far. It was time for me to go home. But I didn't.

Within half an hour watching the movie, my classmate told me my friend was on the phone. Though I never watched Scarface before, I was so engrossed in the plot. I didn't realize that their phone didn't actually ring. Totally frustrated how she had me waiting so long for her, I ran to the phone demanding an explanation. As he handed me the receiver of the white, mounted, long corded wall phone, I said "Hello" and called her name but there was no response.

Then something weird happened. Her boyfriend grabbed me by my wrist while still holding the receiver and pulled me into his bedroom. So I thought it was an insane joke. I looked at him bewildered and asked him what he was doing. By this time, I wasn't in a jovial mood.

He threw me on the bed, slammed the door and attempted to rape me. We wrestled. It seemed like forever. Back and forth, clenching my knees with all my strength with him prying and fighting to get between.

He had no idea who he was messing with. God's hand was upon me. God and I were the majority.

I yelled out to my classmate who was his brother, but he never responded. Balling my fist, I tried to break the bedroom window. Numerous times I tried to reach the windowpane desperate for anyone to help. All the while my knees were locked like a prison cell door as he tried to pry himself in. But I wasn't letting out, and he wasn't getting in.

But God!

There was no way I was going to allow him to take advantage of me. At that moment, I fought for my dear life. I was like a heavyweight champion fighter with nine years of training. I claimed my victory. As my Bishop, Hezekiah Walker, always says, "And because God is the greatest power, we shall not be defeated."

Fortunate for him, he was not successful. The "brute beast" decided he was not going to quit until he accomplished what he had set out to do. He got up off of me. I assumed the fiasco was over. But no. By the time I tried to jump up and run out the door the ruffian, literally, pushed me back onto the bed and pulled a gun out of the top dresser drawer.

Now you see, born and raised in New York City, I never experienced anything of this magnitude. And I lived in East New York, Brooklyn for twelve years of my life during the 70s and 80s – blackouts, gun rivalry and all occurred in the area but I never experienced it hands on.

But God!

My eyes dilated; my mouth opened, and my heart skipped a beat. I was totally perplexed with the barrel of a gun lodged between my eyes while my knees were still locked. As I looked into this dark, cold, barrel of steel, I stopped fighting, but I started to pray silently. Jesus! Jesus! Jesus! I just kept calling His name.

My life flashed before my eyes. So far, the little time I spent on this earth was consumed with a series of molestation, incest, mutilation, and now this. I was frustrated and overwhelmed with disgust.

Tears started to flow down my face. Not so much because of the barrel of the gun resting between my eyes at the bridge of my nose but because of the experiences thus far. Something must change.

Well, I serve an on time God. As the tears started to flow down my face, the girl's boyfriend raised off of me. Trying to make me feel worthless for not granting his wishes, he snapped at me in his dialect, "Gitup!" Yet relieved, I was crazy enough to want to punch him in his face for disrespecting me, but he still had the gun in his hand.

Furious, I just left the house immediately. Tears streamed down my face as I walked home recollecting the facts of the episode that just took place. I ran into a neighborhood friend. Even though I tried to put on a façade, he read right through me. He wanted to know what happened to me. After continuous prying, he reassured me that he and his boys were going to take care of the situation. Shortly, thereafter, I heard the guy was deported because of drug related charges. Thank God!

Chapter Nine

A WAY OF ESCAPE

There was a period in my life where I was totally confused and clueless and being a teenager intensified it. I was raised with the right principles but there was a disconnect. Not clear on how to deal with things, I would just momentarily escape my present situation and create my own getaways. Looking back, I was selfish. Never did I forewarn my parents. I would just get up and go. Escape. Get away!

As a family, we had moved from New York to Florida, which was beautiful. It took some time for me to adjust. But change is good.

Personally, I had not addressed a plethora of issues in my life. I was exposed to new surroundings yet stuck in my old self. And I wanted out.

It was time for me to enjoy my life. I had given away so much of my youth, a decades worth. So much had happened to me between the ages of five and fifteen.

I love New York. There is no place like it, but Florida seemed so sunny, bright and fresh. But I did not want to only experience that externally but also internally. Honestly, I wasn't sure how to go about it. So I would just go on a voyage.

I would never inform anyone - those I lived with and those I would be heading to. Being a kid, I just expected wherever I showed up there would be safety, and I would be taken care of. But I thank God for those heavenly angels God placed in my path. In my troubled state their doors were always opened, and they would never ask a question. They just appeared genuinely concerned about my well-being.

I would find my way up and down the east coast via Greyhound. As many times I've traveled that route, I should have stock in them, seven years, faithfully.

My mother tried her best to get me various forms of help but it was challenging. You have to understand, I always dealt with the unfortunate and unexpected events in my life physically by myself. During the entire time, I felt no one cared and definitely no one would understand. In my eyes, as a teenager, I didn't care how much education someone had, if they didn't experience what I went through there was no way they would understand how to address my issues.

But God!

He kept me despite my shortcomings. His hand was upon me. He was with me every step of the way.

Chapter Ten

MY MIRACULOUS GIFT

Two years into my marriage, we had a baby girl. You don't understand, like Sarah and Abraham, I had an "Is there anything to hard for God?" moment.

Just twelve to thirteen years prior, doctors told me I would not be able to have children. According to the doctors, all the unnecessary methotrexate, overdose of chemotherapy that brought on the coma should have damaged my womb. But as Eliphaz told Job, "You will decide on a matter, and it will be established for you, and light will shine on your ways." That is exactly what I did. Just like Hannah, I asked God to bless my womb and I will give the child right back to Him. "Call those things that be not, as though they were."

I had a healthy 8 pound 4 ounce 19 1/2 inch baby by natural childbirth. Thank you Lord. I call her my miracle baby.

That was very important to me. I felt that God designed women specifically to birth children and I wanted to at least have one.

Mephibosheth, the son of Jonathan, David's friend, and the grandson of King Saul, had a pertinent role being the last-standing heir to his lineage.

Taken care of by a nurse, when she heard the news of the

murders of his fathers, picked him up and ran but dropped him and he became crippled, lame in both feet.

Tragedy struck his life at a tender age yet he became the father of a son named Mica.

Chapter Eleven

IMPULSE

I had had enough - years of abuse, neglect and utter disrespect. One morning, I just clicked. I decided to make a move, a drastic move. At the time, I drove an Expedition and I packed everything that morning but the balcony. Just paying off the monthly bills, I had nothing but $100 left in my account. I never really made any plans. It was just a spur of the moment. Out of frustration and disgust of the entire situation, my baby and I hit the road.

Never driven long distances, I called my sister who is a veteran of I-95. She told me to take I-95 and keep going north. Taking the fast lane, I pressed the cruise control button and set the speed to 100mph.

Stopping once at a truck pit stop around 2am and not having eaten nor even having had a glass of water, I took a three-hour nap. The joke about that was God allowed my baby to sleep the entire ride. I never heard a sound out of her. It was as if I traveled alone. But God was with us.

I arose just as day was about to break. Having only one hundred dollars to feed the gas guzzler, not making any prior arrangements besides knowing where my final destination would be, I cruise controlled my way north with a two and a half year old passenger.

I paused at the front door of one of heaven's angels, whom I have adopted as my Godmother. She is truly one of the most God-sent human beings on the earth. She took my daughter and me in. But that stay was short lived. The Holy Spirit kept prompting me to go back home. But I did not follow the prompting immediately. Not having slept the previous night, I reluctantly decided to go back.

Just as Hagar fled her dysfunctional household then only to be sent back by an angel, so was I. My sister suggested I take an over the counter drug to stay awake. Unfortunate for me, I got a little over the counter drug -happy and popped to many. Cruising 100 mph in the fast lane, in the wee hours of the morning, with a toddler in the back, I fell asleep behind the wheel.

Upon awakening, it was as if my truck was in slow motion, moving diagonally from the fast lane to the middle lane approaching the slow lane where an eighteen-wheeler was traveling south.

It was nothing but the grace of God. It was like a movie, as I looked in the rear view mirror. Traffic was piled up on one another, hesitating to proceed further, as if the vehicles were waiting to see what was about to happen between the Expedition and the eighteen-wheeler. A massacre! Traveling 100mph on cruise control, overdosed with an over the counter drug, and beside that lacking prior sleep, I would have foolishly killed my daughter and myself.

But God!

Chapter Twelve

DARKEST BEFORE THE DAWN

After a month, I headed back north, only to leave most of the material possessions I previously carried, and came back to my Godmother's doorstep. I acquired employment shortly after, moved, but did not acquire enough to comfortably live in NYC.

Evicted! My landlord suggested I go to the Emergency Assistance Unit (EAU). What is that? After her explanation, I asked her if she expected me to go to a shelter as a disabled three-limb woman with a toddler. She showed some form of remorse, wrote me a letter for EAU officials expressing no vacancy and sent me on my way.

One of the most taunting travels of my life, I rode the train to the border of Manhattan and the Bronx, a side of town I have no knowledge of. I started to question God. What is going on! I could never imagine my life coming down to this and with a child.

Fear of the unknown, I went through the process and ended up in a hotel near Columbia University and Riverside Drive with keys to my own door. Privacy. Go figure. Thank you Lord!

No offense but I envisioned this large gymnasium with a million and one cots, as I was sleeping with one eye open in fear of danger throughout the night. Forget taking a shower. My heart is skipping a beat right now reliving it. I do not know how I made it through.

But God!

Chapter Thirteen

A NEW BEGINNING

Throughout the decades of abuse whether it was molestation, mutilation, incest, rape at gunpoint or the after effects of being a battered wife, left many scars. It would not matter where I was - in the grocery store, singing in the choir, taking a midterm test, bathing, in the congregation listening to a sermon, driving, or at a PTA meeting; wherever, I would get flashbacks. Flashbacks, for those who do not know, are images of the evil acts played repetitively in one's mind. It is an involuntary mental recurrence of past trauma. I can't recall when it started but I knew when it ended, Resurrection Week 2010.

Thank God for mothers. They're the ones who know indefinitely something's wrong, and I had had enough - excruciating migraine headaches all day, everyday, uncontrollable crying to and from work on Mass Transit, and nervous breakdowns in the elevator on my way up to work. That season of my life was just severe and dreadful.

My parents always taught me to pray about a situation and God will do the rest. I could hear my mother at this present moment saying, "Golda, take your burdens to the Lord and leave it there." But this time I had a temporary session with a psychiatrist. She explained to me that the flashbacks, migraines and nervous breakdowns were all factors of posttraumatic stress disorder and if I didn't get this situation resolved quickly I would become a manic-depressive. A who...? What...? The devil is a liar!

Medications were prescribed for me but I do not like drugs, not even an aspirin. Once knowledgeable about my situation, I did my own research on how to naturally heal.

In the mean while, I went for my regular physical and two separate doctors, unaware of each other, told me they have done all that they could do and if I don't get my health in check I will leave my eight year old daughter motherless. What a wake up call!

At that time, I had skyrocketed to the heaviest I have ever been. THREE HUNDRED AND TWENTY-FIVE POUNDS. Say what? I have never seen these numbers on the scale, ever before, not even when I was pregnant with my daughter.

O God! O God! If ever there was a time I needed you, it's now. As David cried, "Don't let me down when I run to you, use all your skill to put me together; I wait to see your finished product."

Spiritually, physically and emotionally, I was deteriorating. I was a sneeze away from having a massive stroke and dying.

I knew myself well enough to know how I function best. And at the end of the day, God had to get the glory. Anyone who knows me is aware that I love to praise God; I love to worship and dwell in His presence. That's where I find my strength, peace, joy, His love, and clarity of mind, to say the least. So, if you ever see me give out a shout, do a dance, break out in song or call on His name, let me do so. That's just my coping mechanism. I've come a long way from emotional eating.

You could never have told me at the tender age of twelve that I would lose the life of my arm then at thirteen lose the limb in its entirety.

You could never have told me that, in the same year, I would lose my speech and the movement of my remaining members due to episodes of a coma.

You could never have told me that death would have knocked on my door several times whether by a loaded gun, by the hand of a spouse or by making foolish decisions from behind a wheel. So any chance I get I give God praise.

Just try to understand. What I've been through in the developing stages of my youth alone could have placed me in the crazy house. But the Lord restored my wealth (my worth, security) and happiness and gave me twice as much as before.

But God!

One day I was sitting in my living room just staring off into space, drifting away. My daughter asked me if I was okay. Realizing what was really going on, I had to snap out that, shake myself off and gather my composure. There was no way I was going to allow my daughter to see me in that state.

Shortly after, my mother calls. Before I could say anything, she says, "What's going on?" By the time I started to express myself and find words to explain what I was experiencing, she told me to pack my bags. She was booking a flight.

For three weeks, my daughter and I enjoyed a getaway across the pond, a well-deserved trip, and a life changing experience!

Upon arrival, I developed a praise and worship agenda. As I watched the Christian networks, God led me to this pastor. I never heard of him before but he caught my attention. He offered a weeklong invitation to pray violently.

Violent prayer? He said this Resurrection Week of 2010, we are going to shake foundations, break chains, bind the enemy, and walls are going to fall down. I started to leap in my mother's living room, touching and agreeing with the pastor. At that point, I knew God's hand was on this trip.

Faithfully, I would attend the services as I experienced a change. There was a liberty and a freedom beyond measure as I declared and decreed the Word of the Lord, not only by me speaking it aloud but also having fellow saints charge the atmosphere as a corporate body. It was a sound. It was a shout. I could image the Israelites around the walls of Jericho. I thank God for using that Pastor during that pertinent time in my life.

It did not end there. Another Pastor also had good old-fashioned worship, singing songs of old that took me back to my roots. It was just what my spirit yearned.

HAVE YOU EVER HAD A "BUT GOD" MOMENT?

We all have experienced a "But God" moment. It is anytime you have been healed, delivered or restored from a situation that only a miraculous or supernatural force could carry out.

- ✧ After getting a checkup, the doctor informs you that a procedure must be performed. You get a second opinion and the doctors cannot find the ailment or dis-ease. But God!
- ✧ You are about to be evicted or experience a possible repossession but somehow you get a last minute bonus at work. But God!
- ✧ You leave the gas on or the baby's playing with an unsecured socket yet everyone and everything is safe. But God!
- ✧ Going about your day, running errands, and by inches you miss a metal object falling from a construction site. But God!

The list could go on. What is your "But God" moment? I'd like to know.

ABOUT THE AUTHOR

A woman of distinction, not a victim of circumstance, Golda Hawthorne has turned trauma to triumph. Overcoming her challenges and hardships testify of the power and goodness of the Lord.

Walking under the anointing of a preacher and teacher, with the heart of a true worshipper, a melodious voice and a captivating smile, she will warm your heart.

Founder and CEO of Hawthorne House Inc., she E.M.P.O.W.E.R. 2 I.M.P.A.C.T. others holistically to reach their full potential.

As Borough Director of *Not On My Watch! Safe Haven Network Int'l: A NYC Faith-Based Coalition Against Human Trafficking and Domestic Violence*, she facilitate workshops and train houses of worship to join the movement.

Printed in the United States
By Bookmasters